CW00517620

AUTISM AND I

THE AUTISTIC BOY
In the UNRULY Body

Written By
Gregory C Tino

Illustrated By
Patittoo

Cover Design By
Daniel Petrof

Book Design By
Lori Hayes

ISBN: 9798840583333

I dedicate this book to my family
for their fierce love, support, and perseverance
to get me to where I am today.

FOREWARD

Every kid needs a role model - someone to look up to, someone encouraging, someone who understands, someone who will cheer you on. Many autistic kids, particularly those who are nonspeaking, don't have someone who looks, sounds and communicates like they do to admire. Gregory Tino is that someone they have been seeking! As a nonspeaking adult who worked to manage his unruly body and find a voice, Gregory draws from his lived experience to share his own story of strength, hope and acceptance for autistic and apraxic children. Adults may learn a thing or two as well.

*– **Elizabeth Vosseller***
Executive Director, I-ASC
International Association for Spelling as Communication

PREFACE

I am a nonspeaking autistic person who learned to communicate at age twenty five by pointing to letters on a letterboard using the *Spelling To Communicate* method. I am finally able to let people know that I have apraxia, a common disorder in autism, which makes me unable to form words to communicate and have difficulty with purposeful movement.

I am as intelligent as everyone else, but I was viewed as having the mind of a toddler for many years. Communicating with my voice is not possible for me, but I am able to write beautiful things with my letterboard. As a matter of fact, autism and I wrote this entire book using my letterboard, in the first of what I hope are many books to come in my *"Autism and I"* series.

The message I want to share is that autistics are smart and capable yet underestimated on a daily basis. The apraxic body betrays us, not our mind. Often my body does the opposite of what I want it to.

Since mastering the letterboard I am finding an improved connection between my mind and my body. Today I am proud of my autism and hope to help others by raising awareness of the often misunderstood autistic body.

Gregory C Tino

The moment you accept yourself, you grow.

- *Xan Oku*

The autistic boy was mad.

He was frustrated
with his unruly body.

It would not cooperate
with him.

it said,
"NO!"

When he wanted it to sit still,
it WRIGGLED all around.

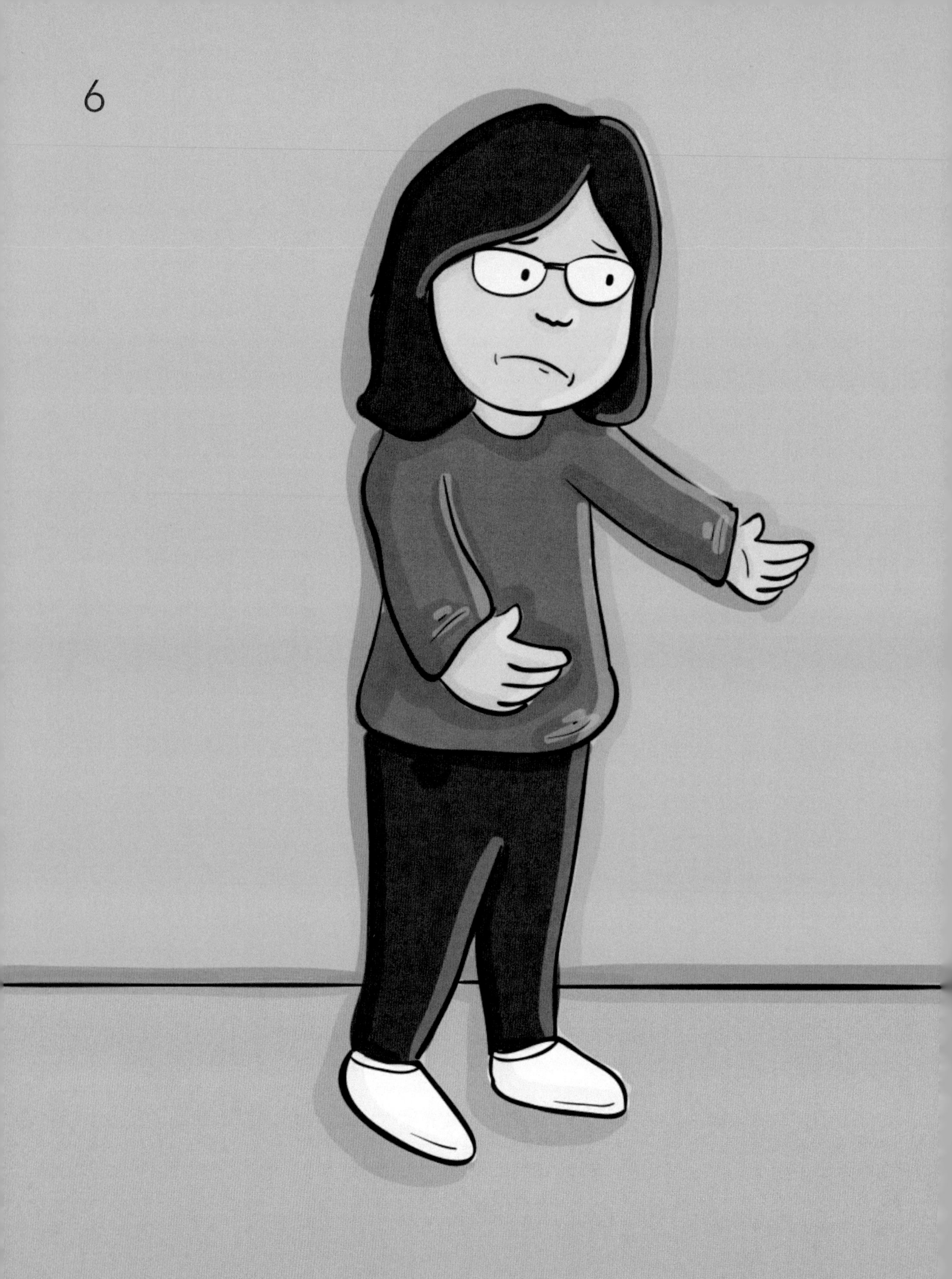

When he wanted to hug his mom, it would *RUN* out of the room.

"*This body needs to GO!*"
thought the boy.

So he shed his body
and went looking
for another one.

First,
he came across
a turtle's body...

and he jumped in.

That was a mistake!

The turtle's body was too slow, and he couldn't get anywhere on time.

Next, he came across
a snake's body...

and he jumped in.

That was another mistake!

The snake's body had no arms,
and he couldn't hug his mom.

Next he came
upon a walrus's body...

and he jumped in.

That was another mistake!

The walrus's body was big and clumsy and no better than his own.

"*This isn't working!*"
thought the boy.

"*Autism has made my body
difficult to control, but it is a
good, strong, healthy body,
so I will try to learn to live with it.*"

So the boy worked hard
and trained his body
to start listening to him.

Eventually it got better.

The boy learned to control his body better, and *finally* was able to give his mom a big hug!

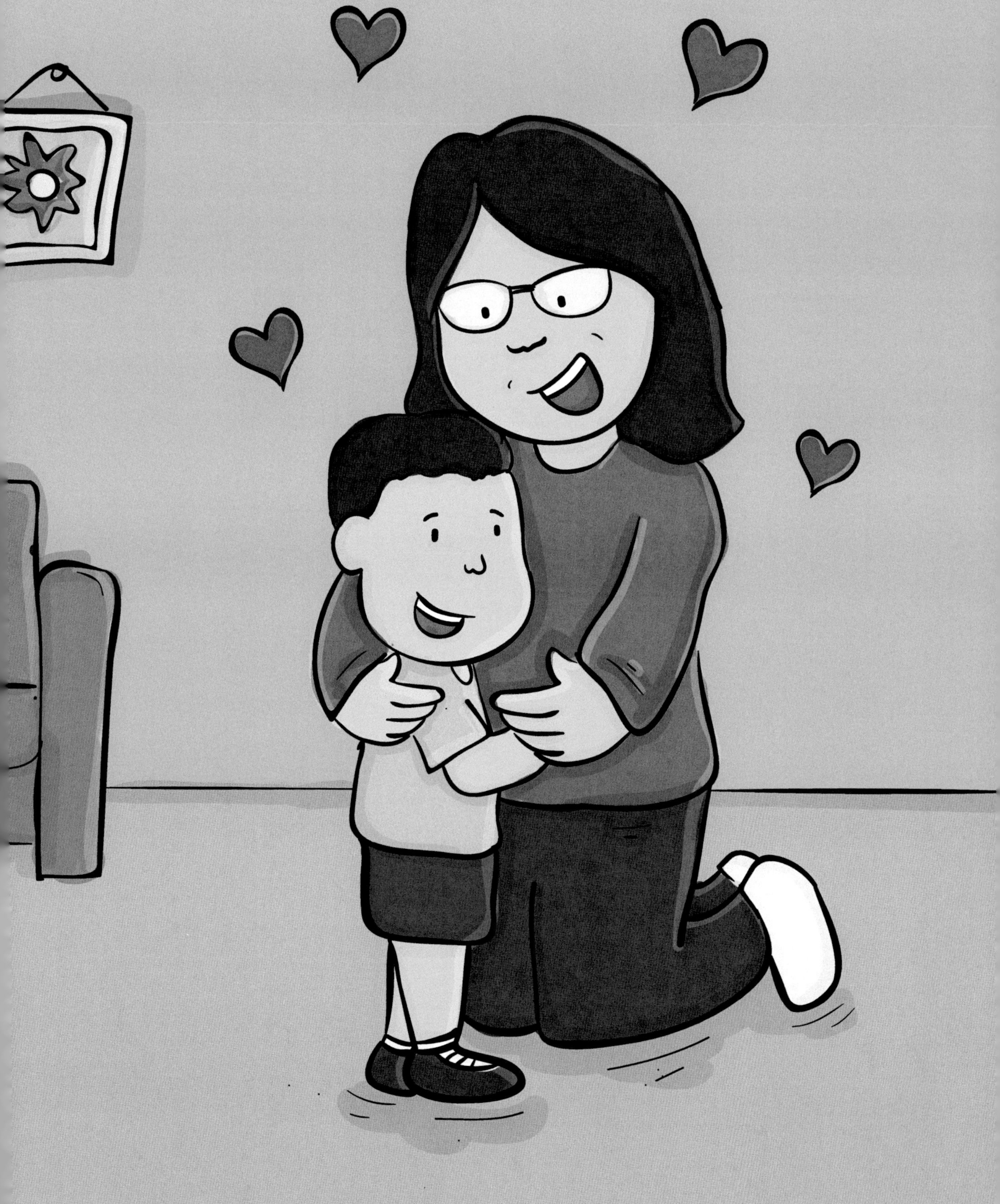

Yes, autism has it's challenges…

but it's *WAY* better
than being a walrus!

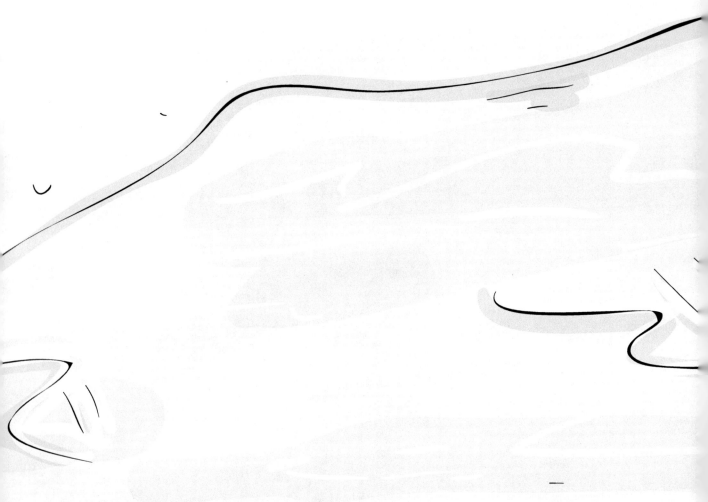

ABOUT THE AUTHOR

Gregory Tino is a nonspeaking autistic who spells on a letterboard to communicate. He is an advocate for other nonspeakers, presents at conferences, and his goal is to educate people on the incredible capabilities of people with autism.

He has written two other books: *The Land Called Boring* and *The Autistic Mind Finally Speaks*. He also has written the narrative for multiple videos on his Youtube channel: **Gregory C Tino.**

In his free time he enjoys writing for his blog, *The Autistic Mind Finally Speaks* on WordPress, spending time with family, and riding his bike.

WHAT IS SPELLING TO COMMUNICATE

Spelling to Communicate teaches individuals with motor challenges purposeful motor skills necessary to point to letters to spell as an alternative means of communication (AAC). The goal is to achieve synchrony between the brain and body.

Skilled and rigorously trained communication partners teach purposeful motor skills using a hierarchy of verbal and gestural prompts.

As motor skills improve through consistent practice, students progress from pointing to letters on letterboards to spell, to typing on a keyboard. Accordingly, communication moves from concrete to abstract as motor skills progress.

FOR MORE INFORMATION
ON SPELLING TO COMMUNICATE

International Association
for Spelling as Communication

https://i-asc.org

(703) 454-0202

&

Inside Voice

www.aalive.org

(484) 471-3335

AVAILABLE ON AMAZON

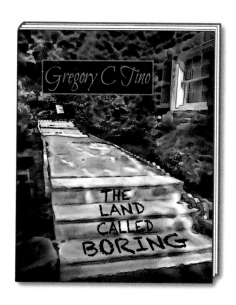

The Land Called Boring

In Gregory Tino's first book, *The Land Called Boring*, Gregory takes us on his journey to finding his voice after years of silence. Illustrated beautifully with pictures of Gregory himself, it is a touching book for all ages.

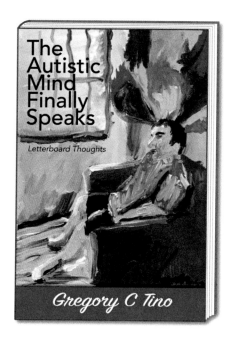

The Autistic Mind Finally Speaks
Letterboard Thoughts

In Gregory Tino's second book, *The Autistic Mind Finally Speaks*, he reveals everything you ever wanted to know about autism but were afraid to ask. It is much different than you ever knew. Wonderfully illustrated by four of Gregory's nonspeaking peers, it is not to be missed.

Made in the USA
Las Vegas, NV
11 August 2022

53084129R00031